# EXPLORE TOGETHER

## TOGETHER

### Resource Book

Copyright © Scripture Union
First published 2017
ISBN 978 1 78506 567 5

British Library Cataloguing-in-Publication Data: a catalogue record of this book is available from the British Library.

Printed in India by Nutech Print Services – India

Cover and internal design by Jake Howe.

Scripture Union is an international Christian charity working with churches in more than 130 countries.
Thank you for purchasing this resource. Any profits from this book support SU in England and Wales to bring the good news of Jesus Christ to children, young people and families and to enable them to meet God through the Bible and prayer.

Find out more about our work and how you can get involved at:
www.scriptureunion.org.uk (England and Wales)
www.suscotland.org.uk (Scotland)
www.suni.co.uk (Northern Ireland)
www.scriptureunion.org (USA)
www.su.org.au (Australia)

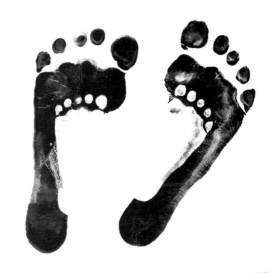

# Contents

# How to... Explore Together

Within our faith communities there is a rich diversity of God's people, all at different stages in their faith development and spiritual experience, and all with different learning needs and preferences. We are a beautiful collection of artists, scholars, reflectors, dancers, data collectors, fact finders, readers, sculptors, writers, musicians, actors, talkers and listeners.

Explore Together places the Bible at the centre of this diversity. It is a new and practical tool for helping people to explore God's Word and hear his voice in a way that embraces their natural preferences. It encourages the community to come together to share their thoughts, questions and revelations with each other. Any and all are welcome and there are no barriers to participation.

At the heart of Explore Together is a desire to see people hear from God and learn more of his love for them. It works with big groups, small groups, mixed-age groups, single-age groups, older people, young people, children, families, house groups, church congregations, youth groups, school groups... In fact, Explore Together can be used in any environment with any group dynamic. It is grounded in years of research and tried and tested in a multitude of contexts.

This resource book is designed to equip you and your community as you adventure, journey and grow with God. On this page and the next we have a few suggestions on how to get the most out of the 12 sessions in this resource and how to use the accompanying resources on the Explore Together website (www.exploretogether.org).

Three more Explore Together resource books are also available, each with 12 sessions on a variety of themes.

## The six steps

There are six essential steps to an Explore Together session, each of which can be tailored to slot into any existing structure and space:

1  **Prepare**
2  **Presenting the Bible**
3  **Pray**
4  **Explore**
5  **Share**
6  **Giving thanks**

These steps are explained in detail in each session outline.

Step 4 provides an opportunity for people to engage with God's Word using the Explore Together questions and the six Explore Together zones. Each zone has been carefully designed to cater for particular learning needs and preferences:

 Colour Zone –
for those who learn by seeing

 Listening Zone –
for those who learn by hearing

 Chat Zone –
for those who learn by thinking aloud

 Word Zone –
for those who learn by reading

 Busy Zone –
for those who learn by doing

 Quiet Zone –
for those who learn by reflecting

Individuals can choose to spend all of their exploring time in one zone, but may also choose to visit several zones, depending upon their preferences. There is no right or wrong amount of time to spend in a zone.

It is quite deliberate that no specific instructions are provided for each zone. Individuals are free to engage however they like with the resources provided in each area as they consider the Explore Together questions for the session.

## Basic kit

Although every Explore Together session is different, there are some common elements that are always included. We will refer to these as the 'basic kit' for Explore Together. Before running your first session we advise that you acquire the following items, and top them up as required:

- Explore Together zone signs (available from www.exploretogether.org)
- Explore Together background soundtrack (available from www.exploretogether.org)
- MP3 players (or the means to play downloaded MP3 tracks – eg CDs and CD player)
- plasticine, play dough or clay
- plastic building bricks
- junk modelling items
- pipe cleaners
- pens, pencils and paper
- coloured pencils/pens
- coloured chalk sticks
- pastels/crayons
- glue, sticky tape
- scissors (child-safe)
- masking tape
- white paper
- black paper
- paper of different sorts, sizes and colours
- manuscript paper
- squared paper
- lined paper
- sticky notes
- a selection of Bible commentaries
- a selection of Bibles (different translations)
- children's Bibles and Bible story books, eg *The Big Bible Storybook* (Scripture Union, 2007)
- chairs/cushions/beanbags
- a separate area where people can be quiet

Each session will need a selection of other resources, detailed in Step 1. Many multimedia resources for each session are available for free from www.exploretogether.org/downloads (using the code from the bottom of page 32).

## Gathering a team

Although it is entirely possible to lead an Explore Together session alone, it is much more effective when there is a team of people working together to share the responsibility and to model involvement. Strategically placed active participants will encourage others to participate.

The colour, word and busy zones benefit from having a carefully placed team member present to keep the focus on the questions, to engage in the zone activity and to draw people into the questions without dominating. The chat zone requires an experienced host to keep everyone focused.

For detailed team member role descriptions visit www.exploretogether.org.

## FAQs

If you have any further questions, it's likely we've answered them in our FAQ section on pages 30 to 32 at the back of this book. If not, please don't hesitate to get in touch via the Scripture Union website: www.scriptureunion.org.uk.

If you'd like to know more about the ideas that underpin Explore Together and hear about our experiences of Explore Together in action, please read our companion book:

**Explore Together: The Journey**

5

# God our provider

*Exodus 16:1–36; 17:1–7*

Themes: meeting needs, prayer, following, gratefulness, glory, obedience, questioning, trust

Sometimes it's hard to trust in God to provide for our every need. The Israelites experienced this, too, when they were hungry and thirsty in the desert. But God did provide – will you trust that he will provide for you, too?

## Prepare

**Resources required**

- 'God our provider' prayer
- 'Living in the desert' audio recording (from *The Big Bible Storybook* audio book)
- 'Living in the desert' story text (from *The Big Bible Storybook*)
- 'God our provider' image collection
- 'God our provider' word collection
- Exodus 16:1–36; 17:1–7 (CEV)
- 'God our provider' Explore Together questions (PDF and PowerPoint)

All available from www.exploretogether.org/downloads (using the code from the bottom of page 32).

You will also need to gather:

- lengths of coloured ribbon or string
- audio versions of different translations of Exodus 16:1–36; 17:1–7
- someone to share a short testimony about how they have seen God's provision in their life
- dictionaries
- disposable cups
- palm-sized smooth pebbles
- items from the Explore Together basic kit (see page 5)

## Presenting the Bible

With the community gathered together, begin by sharing the words from Exodus 16:1–36; 17:1–7. Consider carefully which version of the Bible you choose to read from.

Alternatively or in addition you may choose to use a video re-telling of this story, such as 'Moses in the Wilderness' by Saddleback Kids (https://youtu.be/ogfVBP35U-U).

Without being tempted to answer them, introduce the following questions to your community for them to consider:

- **What does this story teach you about God?**
- **How can you trust God more?**
- **How do you think the Israelites felt in this story?**
- **What do you want to say to God today?**

## Pray

Pray for and with your community, asking God to help you hear from him. This time of prayer can be creative, interactive, responsive, meditative or sung. It could also include Communion and intercession. Ensure that there is a place set aside where people can go if they feel that they need someone to pray with them specifically. Have a small team of people available to offer prayer if required. Prayer ministry should be available throughout an Explore Together session.

You might like to use the 'God our provider' prayer with your community at this point in your gathering.

# Explore

Read out your questions from Step 2 again or display them on a screen. Remind your community to consider these questions as they separate into their explore zones. Some may choose to consider all the questions while others may focus on just one. Some may completely ignore the questions and just open themselves up to God.

Invite your community to separate into small groups, around the zone(s) of their preference. Explain that individuals are welcome to spend as much or as little time in each zone as they wish, engaging at whatever level they feel comfortable. Depending upon where your quiet zone is located, you may wish to provide directions and remind people not to disturb one another when using this space.

### Colour Zone
- coloured chalk
- a roll of black paper
- wax crayons
- marker pens
- large sheets of white paper
- 'Jonah' image collection
- copies of the 'Jonah' ET questions

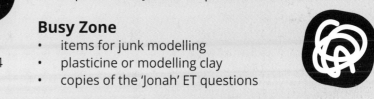

### Listening Zone
- MP3 players or other suitable equipment to play audio files
- 'Jonah obeys God' audio recording (from *The Big Bible Storybook* audio book)
- audio versions of different translations of Jonah 4
- 'In a sulk with God' podcast
- copies of the 'Jonah' ET questions

### Chat Zone
- a separate area with chairs, cushions or beanbags
- a chat zone host who is willing to read the passage again and then lead a discussion around the questions
- copies of Jonah 4 (CEV) or Bibles
- copies of the 'Jonah' ET questions

### Word Zone
- sticky notes
- squared paper
- pens, pencils, paper
- biblical commentaries relating to Jonah 4
- 'Jonah' word collection
- 'Jonah obeys God' story text
- children's Bibles and Bible story books containing a version of Jonah 4
- copies of Jonah 4 (CEV) or Bibles
- copies of the 'Jonah' ET questions

### Busy Zone
- items for junk modelling
- plasticine or modelling clay
- copies of the 'Jonah' ET questions

### Quiet Zone
- a separate area where people can be alone with their thoughts and God
- 'Jonah' image collection (optional)
- copies of Jonah 4 (CEV) or Bibles
- copies of the 'Jonah' ET questions

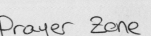

Prayer Zone

# Share

As your time for exploring together draws to a close, invite your community to come back together into small groups of three to five. Suggest that they share their responses to the questions posed at the beginning.

# Giving thanks

Invite the explorers to share their reflections with the wider community, drawing together their responses and noting any common themes that emerge. Conclude by reading Jonah 4 again (from the same Bible version used earlier). Then lead your community in a prayer, thanking God for all that he has revealed through this story. Encourage your community to continue their conversations about this story as they leave, and to take with them any artwork/writings/thoughts from the session.

# Bear good fruit

*Matthew 7:13–23*

Themes: fruitfulness, choices, prayer, spiritual gifts, wisdom, trust, discipleship, commitment, humility, authority

A good tree bears good fruit; a bad tree bears bad fruit – it seems an obvious statement. But how can we make sure that our lives are rooted in Christ and bear the best fruit possible?

## Prepare

**Resources required**
- 'Get real' podcast
- 'Doing things God's way' prayer
- 'Bear good fruit' image collection
- 'Bear good fruit' word collection
- Matthew 7:13–23 (CEV)
- 'Bear good fruit' Explore Together questions (PDF and PowerPoint)

All available from www.exploretogether.org/downloads (using the code from the bottom of page 32).

You will also need to gather:
- twigs from trees
- audio versions of different translations of Matthew 7:13–23
- seeds, compost and small plant pots
- bowls of fruit for people to eat (consider allergies and hygiene issues)
- items from the Explore Together basic kit (see page 5)

## Presenting the Bible

With the community gathered together, begin by sharing the words from Matthew 7:13–23. Consider carefully which version of the Bible you choose to read from.

Without being tempted to answer them, introduce the following questions to your community for them to consider:

- **How can you make sure your life bears good fruit?**
- **What word or sentence strikes you from this passage today?**
- **What do you want to say to Jesus?**
- **What do you need to do to help you grow closer to God?**

## Pray

Pray for and with your community, asking God to help you hear from him. This time of prayer can be creative, interactive, responsive, meditative or sung. It could also include Communion and intercession. Ensure that there is a place set aside where people can go if they feel that they need someone to pray with them specifically. Have a small team of people available to offer prayer if required. Prayer ministry should be available throughout an Explore Together session.

You might like to use the 'Doing things God's way' prayer with your community at this point in your gathering.

# Explore

Read out your questions from Step 2 again or display them on a screen. Remind your community to consider these questions as they separate into their explore zones. Some may choose to consider all the questions while others may focus on just one. Some may completely ignore the questions and just open themselves up to God.

Invite your community to separate into small groups, around the zone(s) of their preference. Explain that individuals are welcome to spend as much or as little time in each zone as they wish, engaging at whatever level they feel comfortable. Depending upon where your quiet zone is located, you may wish to provide directions and remind people not to disturb one another when using this space.

### Colour Zone
- coloured paper
- scissors
- pens and pencils
- 'Bear good fruit' image collection
- twigs from trees
- copies of the 'Bear good fruit' ET questions

### Listening Zone
- MP3 players or suitable equipment to play audio files
- audio versions of different translations of Matthew 7:13–23
- 'Get real' podcast
- copies of the 'Bear good fruit' ET questions

### Chat Zone
- a separate area with chairs, cushions or beanbags
- a chat zone host who is willing to read the passage again and then lead a discussion around the questions
- copies of Matthew 7:13–23 (CEV) or Bibles
- copies of the 'Bear good fruit' ET questions

### Word Zone

- pens, pencils, paper
- biblical commentaries relating to Matthew 7:13–23
- 'Bear good fruit' word collection
- children's Bibles and Bible story books containing a version of Matthew 7:13–23
- copies of Matthew 7:13–23 (CEV) or Bibles
- copies of the 'Bear good fruit' ET questions

### Busy Zone
- play dough or plasticine
- seeds, compost and small plant pots
- bowls of fruit for people to eat (consider allergies and hygiene issues)
- copies of the 'Bear good fruit' ET questions

### Quiet Zone
- a separate area where people can be alone with their thoughts and God
- 'Bear good fruit' image collection (optional)
- copies of Matthew 7:13–23 (CEV) or Bibles
- copies of the 'Bear good fruit' ET questions

# Share

As your time for exploring together draws to a close, invite your community to come back together into small groups of three to five. Suggest that they share their responses to the questions posed at the beginning.

# Giving thanks

Invite the explorers to share their reflections with the wider community, drawing together their responses and noting any common themes that emerge. Conclude by reading Matthew 7:13–23 again (from the same Bible version used earlier). Then lead your community in a prayer, thanking God for all that he has revealed through this story. Encourage your community to continue their conversations about this story as they leave, and to take with them any artwork/writings/thoughts from the session.

# Hear what I say

*Matthew 26:17–35*

Themes: listening, sacrifice, Last Supper, Communion, Passover, fellowship, covenant

This session will help your community to explore the special meal that Jesus shared with his friends. If you are able, and it suits your context, it would be especially appropriate to celebrate Holy Communion as part of this session.

## Prepare

**Resources required**
- 'Listening' prayer
- 'The Lord's Supper' podcast
- 'A meal with Jesus' audio recording (from *The Big Bible Storybook* audio book)
- 'Hear what I say' image collection
- 'Hear what I say' word collection
- Matthew 26:17–35 (CEV)
- 'Hear what I say' Explore Together questions (PDF and PowerPoint)

All available from www.exploretogether.org/downloads (using the code from the bottom of page 32).

You will also need to gather:
- water-based paint for wax-resist pictures, brushes
- white wax candles for drawing
- coloured small paper squares for making mosaics
- audio versions of different translations of Matthew 26:17–35
- connecting building blocks, including small people figures
- origami paper
- instructions for making origami cup or goblet (search online)
- items from the Explore Together basic kit (see page 5)

## Presenting the Bible

With the community gathered together, begin by sharing the words from Matthew 26:17–35. Consider carefully which version of the Bible you choose to read from.

Alternatively or in addition you may choose to read the passage from a dramatised version of the Bible or present it as a drama with a team of volunteers.

Without being tempted to answer them, introduce the following questions to your community for them to consider:

- **What have you heard about this story today that is new to you?**
- **Why was it important for Jesus' friends to hear what he had to say?**
- **Why is it important for you to hear what Jesus has to say?**
- **How does this story make you feel?**

## Pray

Pray for and with your community, asking God to help you hear from him. This time of prayer can be creative, interactive, responsive, meditative or sung. It could also include Communion and intercession. Ensure that there is a place set aside where people can go if they feel that they need someone to pray with them specifically. Have a small team of people available to offer prayer if required. Prayer ministry should be available throughout an Explore Together session.

You may also like to use the 'Listening' prayer to help your community pray together at this time.

# Explore

Read out your questions from Step 2 again or display them on a screen. Remind your community to consider these questions as they separate into their explore zones. Some may choose to consider all the questions while others may focus on just one. Some may completely ignore the questions and just open themselves up to God.

Invite your community to separate into small groups, around the zone(s) of their preference. Explain that individuals are welcome to spend as much or as little time in each zone as they wish, engaging at whatever level they feel comfortable. Depending upon where your quiet zone is located, you may wish to provide directions and remind people not to disturb one another when using this space.

## Colour Zone
- water-based paint for wax-resist pictures, brushes
- white paper
- white wax candles for drawing
- coloured small paper squares for making mosaics
- glue
- 'Hear what I say' image collection
- copies of the 'Hear what I say' ET questions

## Listening Zone
- MP3 players, or other suitable equipment to play audio recordings
- 'A meal with Jesus' audio recording (from *The Big Bible Storybook* audio book)
- audio versions of different translations of Matthew 26:17–35
- 'The Lord's Supper' podcast
- copies of the 'Hear what I say' ET questions

## Chat Zone
- a separate area with chairs, cushions or beanbags
- a chat zone host who is willing to read the passage again and then lead a discussion around the questions
- copies of Matthew 26:17–35 (CEV) or Bibles
- copies of the 'Hear what I say' ET questions

## Word Zone
- pens, pencils, paper
- biblical commentaries relating to Matthew 26:17–35
- 'Hear what I say' word collection
- copies of *The Big Bible Storybook* open at 'A meal with Jesus', or other children's Bibles and Bible story books containing a version of Matthew 26:17–35
- copies of Matthew 26:17–35 (CEV) or Bibles
- copies of the 'Hear what I say' ET questions

## Busy Zone
- plasticine or play dough
- connecting building blocks, including small people figures
- origami paper
- instructions for making origami cup or goblet
- copies of the 'Hear what I say' ET questions

## Quiet Zone
- a separate area where people can be alone with their thoughts and God
- 'Hear what I say' image collection (optional)
- copies of Matthew 26:17–35 (CEV) or Bibles
- copies of the 'Hear what I say' ET questions

# Share

As your time for exploring together draws to a close, invite your community to come back together into small groups of three to five. Suggest that they share their responses to the questions posed at the beginning.

# Giving thanks

Invite the explorers to share their reflections with the wider community, drawing together their responses and noting any common themes that emerge. Conclude by reading Matthew 26:17–35 again (from the same Bible version used earlier). Then lead your community in a prayer, thanking God for all that he has revealed through this story. Encourage your community to continue their conversations about this story as they leave, and to take with them any artwork/writings/thoughts from the session.

# Love stories

*Luke 10:25–37*

Themes: love, generosity, compassion, mercy, action, integrity

A very familiar story, the parable of the good Samaritan is often interpreted as something that simply suggests those who follow Jesus should help those in need – but what more can we learn from this story?

# Prepare

**Resources required**
- 'Praying for others' prayer idea
- 'Informed or transformed?' podcast
- 'Jesus tells a story' audio recording (from *The Big Bible Storybook* audio book)
- 'Jesus tells a story' story text (from *The Big Bible Storybook*)
- 'Love stories' image collection
- 'Love stories' word collection
- Luke 10:25–37 (CEV)
- 'Love stories' Explore Together questions (PDF and PowerPoint)

All available from www.exploretogether.org/downloads (using the code from the bottom of page 32).

You will also need to gather:
- YouTube video: www.youtube.com/watch?v=-AxTgnmzZE8
- small pieces of fabric in a variety of colours
- string or ribbon
- audio versions of different translations of Luke 10:25–37
- old newspapers
- sticking plasters and bandages (be aware of allergies)
- items from the Explore Together basic kit (see page 5)

# Presenting the Bible

With the community gathered together, begin by sharing the words from Luke 10:25–37. Consider carefully which version of the Bible you choose to read from.

Alternatively or in addition you may choose to use the following YouTube video as part of your Bible presentation:

www.youtube.com/watch?v=-AxTgnmzZE8

Without being tempted to answer them, introduce the following questions to your community for them to consider:

- **What do you notice in this story that you've never noticed before?**
- **Why does God want you to hear this story today?**
- **Who is your neighbour? And how can you show them the love of Jesus?**
- **What do you want to say to God today?**

# Pray

Pray for and with your community, asking God to help you hear from him. This time of prayer can be creative, interactive, responsive, meditative or sung. It could also include communion and intercession. Ensure that there is a place set aside where people can go if they feel that they need someone to pray with them specifically. Have a small team of people available to offer prayer if required. Prayer ministry should be available throughout an Explore Together session.

You might also like to use the 'Praying for others' prayer idea with your community during this time.

# Explore

Read out your questions from Step 2 again or display them on a screen. Remind your community to consider these questions as they separate into their explore zones. Some may choose to consider all the questions while others may focus on just one. Some may completely ignore the questions and just open themselves up to God.

Invite your community to separate into small groups, around the zone(s) of their preference. Explain that individuals are welcome to spend as much or as little time in each zone as they wish, engaging at whatever level they feel comfortable. Depending upon where your quiet zone is located, you may wish to provide directions and remind people not to disturb one another when using this space.

### Colour Zone
- glue
- scissors
- paper
- wax crayons
- 'Love stories' image collection
- small pieces of fabric in a variety of colours
- string or ribbon
- copies of the 'Love stories' ET questions

### Listening Zone
- MP3 players or other suitable equipment to play audio files
- 'Jesus tells a story' audio recording (from *The Big Bible Storybook* audio book)
- audio versions of different translations of Luke 10:25–37
- 'Informed or transformed?' podcast
- copies of the 'Love stories' ET questions

### Chat Zone
- a separate area with chairs, cushions or beanbags
- a chat zone host who is willing to read the passage again and then lead a discussion around the questions
- copies of Luke 10:25–37 (CEV) or Bibles
- copies of the 'Love stories' ET questions

### Word Zone
- notebooks
- scissors
- glue
- pens, pencils, paper
- biblical commentaries relating to Luke 10:25–37
- 'Love stories' word collection
- 'Jesus tells a story' story text
- other children's Bibles and Bible story books containing a version of Luke 10:25–37
- copies of Luke 10:25–37 (CEV) or Bibles
- old newspapers
- copies of the 'Love stories' ET questions

### Busy Zone
- play dough or plasticine
- building blocks
- sticking plasters and bandages
- copies of the 'Love stories' ET questions

### Quiet Zone
- a separate area where people can be alone with their thoughts and God
- 'Love stories' image collection (optional)
- copies of Luke 10:25–37 (CEV) or Bibles
- copies of the 'Love stories' ET questions

# Share

As your time for exploring together draws to a close, invite your community to come back together into small groups of three to five. Suggest that they share their responses to the questions posed at the beginning.

# Giving thanks

Invite the explorers to share their reflections with the wider community, drawing together their responses and noting any common themes that emerge. Conclude by reading Luke 10:25–37 again (from the same Bible version used earlier). Then lead your community in a prayer, thanking God for all that he has revealed through this story. Encourage your community to continue their conversations about this story as they leave, and to take with them any artwork/writings/thoughts from the session.

# Only Jesus

*John 14:1–14*

Themes: one way, following, discipleship, faith, truth, heaven, eternity, prayer, trust

This session will offer your community a chance to explore some of Jesus' most famous words – 'I am the way and the truth and the life. No one comes to the Father except through me.' (John 14:6). What do these words mean for your community today?

# Prepare

**Resources required**
- 'Only Jesus' prayer
- 'One-way system' podcast
- 'Only Jesus' image collection
- 'Only Jesus' word collection
- John 14:1–14 (CEV)
- 'Only Jesus' Explore Together questions (PDF and PowerPoint)

All available from www.exploretogether.org/downloads (using the code from the bottom of page 32).

You will also need to gather:
- 'One Way Jesus' (Hillsong United, 2004, available at: https://itun.es/gb/0EQeg)
- a roll of white paper
- coloured paper cut into arrow shapes
- glitter
- audio versions of different translations of John 14:1–14
- copies of *The Highway Code*
- a carpet playmat road map with small cars or other vehicles to push around
- items from the Explore Together basic kit (see page 5)

# Presenting the Bible

With the community gathered together, begin by sharing the words from John 14:1–14. Consider carefully which version of the Bible you choose to read from.

Alternatively or in addition you may choose to listen to the song 'One Way Jesus' (Hillsong United, 2004) or perhaps incorporate this into a time of sung worship.

Without being tempted to answer them, introduce the following questions to your community for them to consider:

- **What does it mean to you that Jesus is 'the way, the truth and the life'?**
- **What does Jesus want to say to you today?**
- **How does it feel to know that Jesus has prepared a place for you in heaven?**
- **What do you want to ask God?**

# Pray

Pray for and with your community, asking God to help you hear from him. This time of prayer can be creative, interactive, responsive, meditative or sung. It could also include Communion and intercession. Ensure that there is a place set aside where people can go if they feel that they need someone to pray with them specifically. Have a small team of people available to offer prayer if required. Prayer ministry should be available throughout an Explore Together session.

You might like to use the words of the 'Only Jesus' prayer during this time.

# Explore

Read out your questions from Step 2 again or display them on a screen. Remind your community to consider these questions as they separate into their explore zones. Some may choose to consider all the questions while others may focus on just one. Some may completely ignore the questions and just open themselves up to God.

Invite your community to separate into small groups, around the zone(s) of their preference. Explain that individuals are welcome to spend as much or as little time in each zone as they wish, engaging at whatever level they feel comfortable. Depending upon where your quiet zone is located, you may wish to provide directions and remind people not to disturb one another when using this space.

## Colour Zone
- a roll of white paper
- pens, pencils, and wax crayons
- glue
- 'Only Jesus' image collection
- coloured paper cut into arrow shapes
- glitter
- copies of the 'Only Jesus' ET questions

## Listening Zone
- MP3 players or other suitable equipment to play audio files
- audio versions of different translations of John 14:1–14
- 'One-way system' podcast
- copies of the 'Only Jesus' ET questions

## Chat Zone
- a separate area with chairs, cushions or beanbags
- a chat zone host who is willing to read the passage again and then lead a discussion around the questions
- copies of John 14:1–14 (CEV) or Bibles
- copies of the 'Only Jesus' ET questions

## Word Zone

- pens, pencils, paper
- sticky notes
- biblical commentaries relating to John 14:1–14
- 'Only Jesus' word collection
- Bible story books containing a version of John 14:1–14
- copies of John 14:1–14 (CEV) or Bibles
- copies of *The Highway Code*
- copies of the 'Only Jesus' ET questions

## Busy Zone
- a carpet playmat road map with small cars or other vehicles to push around
- copies of the 'Only Jesus' ET questions

## Quiet Zone
- a separate area where people can be alone with their thoughts and God
- 'Only Jesus' image collection (optional)
- copies of John 14:1–14 (CEV) or Bibles
- copies of the 'Only Jesus' ET questions

# Share

As your time for exploring together draws to a close, invite your community to come back together into small groups of three to five. Suggest that they share their responses to the questions posed at the beginning.

# Giving thanks

Invite the explorers to share their reflections with the wider community, drawing together their responses and noting any common themes that emerge. Conclude by reading John 14:1–14 again (from the same Bible version used earlier). Then lead your community in a prayer, thanking God for all that he has revealed through this story. Encourage your community to continue their conversations about this story as they leave, and to take with them any artwork/writings/thoughts from the session.

# God speaks

## Acts 8:26–40

Themes: guidance, discipleship, listening, mission, good news, Holy Spirit, prophecy, faith, baptism

The Lord speaks to us in many ways. In this story, we see God speaking directly through his Word, but also through Philip's words and actions. How might God want to speak to you?

# Prepare

### Resources required
- 'Philip' audio recording (from *The Big Bible Storybook* audio book)
- 'Guided by God' podcast
- 'Philip' story text (from *The Big Bible Storybook*)
- 'God speaks' image collection
- 'God speaks' word collection
- Acts 8:26–40 (CEV)
- 'God speaks' Explore Together questions (PDF and PowerPoint)

All available from www.exploretogether.org/downloads (using the code from the bottom of page 32).

You will also need to gather:
- 'Word of God speak' (Mercy Me, 2008, available at: https://itun.es/gb/pi3D0)
- audio versions of different translations of Acts 8:26–40
- someone to deliver a short sermon on Acts 8:26–40
- a large world map
- building blocks – including people and wheels
- pipe cleaners
- shallow trays of sand
- items from the Explore Together basic kit (see page 5)

# Presenting the Bible

With the community gathered together, begin by sharing the words from Acts 8:26–40. Consider carefully which version of the Bible you choose to read from.

Alternatively you may choose to have some volunteers act out this story as they walk around your meeting space – representing the distances travelled in the story.

Without being tempted to answer them, introduce the following questions to your community for them to consider:

- **How might God want to speak to you today?**
- **Which part of his word do you want God to help you understand?**
- **How might God want to use you to speak for him?**
- **What do you want to say to God today?**

# Pray

Pray for and with your community, asking God to help you hear from him. This time of prayer can be creative, interactive, responsive, meditative or sung. It could also include Communion and intercession. Ensure that there is a place set aside where people can go if they feel that they need someone to pray with them specifically. Have a small team of people available to offer prayer if required. Prayer ministry should be available throughout an Explore Together session.

# Explore

Read out your questions from Step 2 again or display them on a screen. Remind your community to consider these questions as they separate into their explore zones. Some may choose to consider all the questions while others may focus on just one. Some may completely ignore the questions and just open themselves up to God.

Invite your community to separate into small groups, around the zone(s) of their preference. Explain that individuals are welcome to spend as much or as little time in each zone as they wish, engaging at whatever level they feel comfortable. Depending upon where your quiet zone is located, you may wish to provide directions and remind people not to disturb one another when using this space.

### Colour Zone
- coloured pens
- pencil crayons
- large sheets of white paper
- pastels
- coloured chalks
- 'God speaks' image collection
- copies of the 'God speaks' ET questions

### Listening Zone
- MP3 players or other suitable equipment to play audio files
- 'Philip' audio recording (from *The Big Bible Storybook* audio book)
- audio versions of different translations of Acts 8:26–40
- 'Word of God speak' (Mercy Me, 2008)
- someone to deliver a short sermon on Acts 8:26–40
- copies of the 'God speaks' ET questions

### Chat Zone
- a separate area with chairs, cushions or beanbags
- a chat zone host who is willing to read the passage again and then lead a discussion around the questions
- copies of Acts 8:26–40 (CEV) or Bibles
- copies of the 'God speaks' ET questions

### Word Zone
- pens, pencils, paper
- biblical commentaries relating to Acts 8:26–40
- 'God speaks' word collection
- 'Philip' story text
- children's Bibles and Bible story books containing a version of Acts 8:26–40
- copies of Acts 8:26–40 (CEV) or Bibles
- a large world map
- copies of the 'God speaks' ET questions

### Busy Zone
- building blocks – including people and wheels
- pipe cleaners
- shallow trays of sand
- copies of the 'God speaks' ET questions

### Quiet Zone
- a separate area where people can be alone with their thoughts and God
- 'God speaks' image collection (optional)
- copies of Acts 8:26–40 (CEV) or Bibles
- copies of the 'God speaks' ET questions

# Share

As your time for exploring together draws to a close, invite your community to come back together into small groups of three to five. Suggest that they share their responses to the questions posed at the beginning.

# Giving thanks

Invite the explorers to share their reflections with the wider community, drawing together their responses and noting any common themes that emerge. Conclude by reading Acts 8:26–40 again (from the same Bible version used earlier). Then lead your community in a prayer, thanking God for all that he has revealed through this story. Encourage your community to continue their conversations about this story as they leave, and to take with them any artwork/writings/thoughts from the session.

# Joy in hardship

## *Acts 13:1–52*

Themes: calling, commitment, hard times, commissioning, joy, promise, hope, trust, mission, opposition, persecution

Happiness is never guaranteed in life, but because of Jesus there can be joy even in the most difficult times. This session will help your community to explore these issues in a meaningful way.

# Prepare

**Resources required**

- 'Joy in hardship' diary talk
- 'Paul helps Barnabas' audio recording (from *The Big Bible Storybook* audio book)
- 'New ventures' podcast
- Commissioning prayer
- 'Joy in hardship' image collection
- 'Joy in hardship' word collection
- Acts 13:1–52 (CEV)
- 'Joy in hardship' Explore Together questions (PDF and PowerPoint)

All available from www.exploretogether.org/downloads (using the code from the bottom of page 32).

You will also need to gather:

- marbling ink and trays of water
- audio versions of different translations of Acts 13:1–52
- small model people
- sand in trays
- threads for braiding
- items from the Explore Together basic kit (see page 5)

# Presenting the Bible

With the community gathered together, begin by sharing the words from Acts 13:1–52. Consider carefully which version of the Bible you choose to read from.

In addition you may choose to use the 'Joy in hardship' diary talk before reading your Bible passage.

Without being tempted to answer them, introduce the following questions to your community for them to consider:

- **What can you learn from Paul and Barnabas' experience?**
- **Can you think of any other situations, past and present, where God brings joy in hardship?**
- **How can you remember that Jesus is with you, even throughout the hard times?**
- **What do you want to say to God today?**

# Pray

Pray for and with your community, asking God to help you hear from him. This time of prayer can be creative, interactive, responsive, meditative or sung. It could also include Communion and intercession. Ensure that there is a place set aside where people can go if they feel that they need someone to pray with them specifically. Have a small team of people available to offer prayer if required. Prayer ministry should be available throughout an Explore Together session.

# Explore

Read out your questions from Step 2 again or display them on a screen. Remind your community to consider these questions as they separate into their explore zones. Some may choose to consider all the questions while others may focus on just one. Some may completely ignore the questions and just open themselves up to God.

Invite your community to separate into small groups, around the zone(s) of their preference. Explain that individuals are welcome to spend as much or as little time in each zone as they wish, engaging at whatever level they feel comfortable. Depending upon where your quiet zone is located, you may wish to provide directions and remind people not to disturb one another when using this space.

### Colour Zone
- white paper
- coloured pastels
- 'Joy in hardship' image collection
- marbling ink and trays of water
- copies of the 'Joy in hardship' ET questions

### Listening Zone
- MP3 players or other suitable equipment for playing audio files
- 'Paul helps Barnabas' audio recording (from *The Big Bible Storybook* audio book)
- 'New ventures' podcast
- audio versions of different translations of Acts 13:1–52
- copies of the 'Joy in hardship' ET questions

### Chat Zone
- a separate area with chairs, cushions or beanbags
- a chat zone host who is willing to read the passage again and then lead a discussion around the questions
- copies of Acts 13:1–52 (CEV) or Bibles
- copies of the 'Joy in hardship' ET questions

### Word Zone

- pens, pencils, paper
- biblical commentaries relating to Acts 13:1–52
- 'Joy in hardship' word collection
- copies of *The Big Bible Storybook* open at 'Paul helps Barnabas', or other children's Bibles and Bible story books containing a version of Acts 13:1–52
- copies of Acts 13:1–52 (CEV) or Bibles
- copies of the 'Joy in hardship' ET questions

### Busy Zone

- threads for braiding
- small model people
- sand in trays
- copies of the 'Joy in hardship' ET questions

### Quiet Zone
- a separate area where people can be alone with their thoughts and God
- 'Joy in hardship' image collection (optional)
- copies of Acts 13:1–52 (CEV) or Bibles
- copies of the 'Joy in hardship' ET questions

# Share

As your time for exploring together draws to a close, invite your community to come back together into small groups of three to five. Suggest that they share their responses to the questions posed at the beginning.

# Giving thanks

Invite the explorers to share their reflections with the wider community, drawing together their responses and noting any common themes that emerge. Conclude by reading Acts 13:1–52 again (from the same Bible version used earlier). Then lead your community in a prayer, thanking God for all that he has revealed through this story. Encourage your community to continue their conversations about this story as they leave, and to take with them any artwork/writings/thoughts from the session.

You might also like to use the commissioning prayer.

# When God lives with us

## *Philemon*

Themes: forgiveness, acceptance, love, reconciliation, patience, encouragement

An often overlooked letter gives your community the opportunity to consider their own attitudes towards forgiveness and acceptance. When Paul writes to Philemon, he is asking him to forgive Onesimus and work with him again – forgiveness and acceptance in action! When God dwells in our hearts, these are the kind of qualities that he wants to nurture in us.

# Prepare

**Resources required**
- 'Forgive us' prayer
- 'Philemon 8–16' podcast
- 'Philemon' audio recording (from *The Big Bible Storybook* audio book)
- 'Philemon' story text (from *The Big Bible Storybook*)
- 'When God lives with us' image collection
- 'When God lives with us' word collection
- 'When God lives with us' Explore Together questions (PDF and PowerPoint)
- Philemon (CEV)

All available from www.exploretogether.org/downloads (using the code from the bottom of page 32).

You will also need to gather:
- sticks of charcoal for drawing
- audio versions of different translations of Philemon
- news stories of people who have forgiven others against the odds (search online)
- trays containing various sticky things – such as wallpaper paste, compost, synthetic feathers, glitter, brown paint etc
- bowls of water for handwashing (and a person to keep providing clean water for these)
- paper towels for hand drying
- items from the Explore Together basic kit (see page 5)

# Presenting the Bible

With the community gathered together, begin by sharing the words from Philemon. Consider carefully which version of the Bible you choose to read from.

In addition you may choose to put Paul's letter to Philemon in some sort of context, based on information you can find in most study Bibles and commentaries.

Without being tempted to answer them, introduce the following questions to your community for them to consider:

- **How do you feel about forgiveness?**
- **How does it feel to know that God will always forgive you if you ask him to?**
- **How can you see God at work in your life?**
- **What does God want to say to you today?**

# Pray

Pray for and with your community, asking God to help you hear from him. This time of prayer can be creative, interactive, responsive, meditative or sung. It could also include Communion and intercession. Ensure that there is a place set aside where people can go if they feel that they need someone to pray with them specifically. Have a small team of people available to offer prayer if required. Prayer ministry should be available throughout an Explore Together session.

Alternatively, or in addition you could use the 'Forgive us' prayer provided as part of this session.

# Explore

Read out your questions from Step 2 again or display them on a screen. Remind your community to consider these questions as they separate into their explore zones. Some may choose to consider all the questions while others may focus on just one. Some may completely ignore the questions and just open themselves up to God.

Invite your community to separate into small groups, around the zone(s) of their preference. Explain that individuals are welcome to spend as much or as little time in each zone as they wish, engaging at whatever level they feel comfortable. Depending upon where your quiet zone is located, you may wish to provide directions and remind people not to disturb one another when using this space.

## Colour Zone
- black and white paper
- white chalk
- red paint and brushes
- 'When God lives with us' image collection
- sticks of charcoal for drawing
- copies of the 'When God lives with us' ET questions

## Listening Zone
- MP3 players or other suitable equipment to play audio files
- 'Philemon' audio recording (from *The Big Bible Storybook* audio book)
- audio versions of different translations of Philemon
- 'Philemon 8–16' podcast
- copies of the 'When God lives with us' ET questions

## Chat Zone
- a separate area with chairs, cushions or beanbags
- a chat zone host who is willing to read the passage again and then lead a discussion around the questions
- copies of Philemon (CEV) or Bibles
- copies of the 'When God lives with us' ET questions

## Word Zone
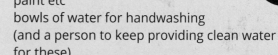
- pens, pencils, paper
- biblical commentaries relating to Philemon
- 'When God lives with us' word collection
- 'Philemon' story text
- other children's Bibles and Bible story books containing a version of Philemon
- copies of Philemon (CEV) or Bibles
- news stories of people who have forgiven others against the odds
- copies of the 'When God lives with us' ET questions

## Busy Zone
- trays containing various sticky things – such as wallpaper paste, compost, synthetic feathers, glitter, brown paint etc
- bowls of water for handwashing (and a person to keep providing clean water for these)
- paper towels for hand drying
- copies of the 'When God lives with us' ET questions

## Quiet Zone

- a separate area where people can be alone with their thoughts and God
- 'When God lives with us' image collection (optional) copies of Philemon (CEV) or Bibles
- copies of the 'When God lives with us' ET questions

# Share

As your time for exploring together draws to a close, invite your community to come back together into small groups of three to five. Suggest that they share their responses to the questions posed at the beginning.

# Giving thanks

Invite the explorers to share their reflections with the wider community, drawing together their responses and noting any common themes that emerge. Conclude by reading Philemon again (from the same Bible version used earlier). Then lead your community in a prayer, thanking God for all that he has revealed through this story. Encourage your community to continue their conversations about this story as they leave, and to take with them any artwork/writings/thoughts from the session.

# Frequently asked questions

**Does Explore Together negate the need for age-specific ministry?**
The practice of Explore Together embodies the principle that a multigenerational community can engage with God's Word, learn from each other and grow together.

It is also true that within age-specific ministries there can be diversity of thought, rich experience and God-given creativity for sharing. Explore Together is a rare tool that can be used to nourish all-age community as well as enhance those ministries aimed at specific age-groups.

Although some churches do take and use Explore Together as a discrete part of their monthly programme, many churches use it to enrich their existing activities. The beauty of Explore Together is that it can be used within children's groups, youth groups, house groups, school groups, Bible study groups, outreach groups or even within the family home – in fact, anywhere that the Bible is shared. Its benefits are not restricted to all-age services.

**We are a very traditional church community. How could Explore Together work within our traditions?**
Explore Together embraces tradition but also pushes the boundaries that can be imposed by those traditions. It can fit neatly into the traditional order of things and can also be the catalyst that takes the community on an additional adventure.

Explore Together can be used to help people understand and interpret the meaning and value of symbol and tradition. A whole range of churches from a number of different traditions have taken and used it in different ways. It offers flexibility for churches and communities to make the time of exploring their own, using it so that it fits their group of people.

**Our church has many people/a few people. Will it work here?**
Over the last five years we have seen Explore Together used in small groups with only a few individuals and also in larger settings. We have known Explore Together to be used within a family home, and also within a programme at Spring Harvest for 450 children.

Key to the smooth running of Explore Together is preparation and planning. It is important to consider how the participants will arrange themselves into small groups. There is a danger that individuals who are close friends, or of similar age and background, will organise themselves into groups, therefore missing out on the excellent opportunity to learn from those who are a different age or stage in their lives. Inclusivity is key if individuals want to be challenged to learn something new.

While the planning, organisation and setting up of the zones are essential, large or small numbers of people do not present a challenge. No matter how large the group is, Step 5: Share is always done in small groups of three to five people. When feeding back in larger churches or groups, having a group of people with roving radio microphones in the congregation works very well.

**Isn't Explore Together a bit chaotic, especially with children present?**
It is chaotic in the sense that everyone is engaging in different ways, but not because the children are present. The explore zones are designed to embrace a range of learning preferences. Individuals of all ages very quickly find their own preferred activity and become occupied. Although there might be a buzz in the room, activity will be purposeful, colourful and appealing, and everyone has the freedom to move around and make choices in a safe and supportive environment. Many adults find the kinaesthetic dimension of Explore Together appealing too!

**Does Explore Together need a lot of space? We have fixed pews in our church building that often restrict what we can do**
Explore Together can be planned carefully to fit flexibly into spaces that are different in size and organised in different ways. The explore zones do not all need to happen in one room; they could be spread out to happen in different areas. Your choice of activities can also be tailored to the amount of space you have, and you can creatively use the edges

and corners of a room that contains pews. The smallest setting for Explore Together that we have heard about is at a dining room table in a family home.

## I find sharing my ideas and thoughts very daunting. Do I really have to share my answers? Will others pressure me into talking?

The value of small groups is significant. Individuals have the opportunity to share what they have discovered, and shape the views, thinking and experiences of each other.

It is important that small groups are 'safe places', and that key expectations for how those groups will function are shared. Small groups need to be a place where individuals might not speak. There is huge value in being part of a small group and simply listening. Small groups also need to be a place where people can freely make mistakes, a place where original thoughts and ideas are encouraged. Some individuals might benefit from talking their ideas through one-to-one with another before sharing in a group, but others may never do so.

Individuals within groups need to be careful not to add to pressure others might feel. It should never be an expectation that everyone will talk.

## Is Explore Together an alternative to Messy Church?

Messy Church and Explore Together complement each other in many ways. Explore Together can be used as a way of engaging with the Bible within any context. It is just one way of exploring the Bible 'in community'.

Messy Church is a Fresh Expression of church developed to encourage new congregations previously out of reach of 'traditional' church. Rather than replace Messy Church, Explore Together could be used within a Messy Church congregation. In his book *Making Disciples in Messy Church*, Paul Moore mentions that there is a lack of discipleship resources specifically designed for adults and children to use together in an all-age context, like Messy Church, or in the family home. I would strongly suggest that Explore Together ticks that box.

## How inclusive is Explore Together for individuals with disabilities and learning difficulties?

Individuals with disabilities and learning difficulties have been involved in Explore Together since its inception. Those with physical difficulties, Down syndrome, diagnoses of ADHD and autistic spectrum conditions have all participated. Individuals are able to express their personal skills, interests and abilities in the explore zone. They can focus on tasks for a length of time that fits their capabilities, and they can share their answers in verbal and nonverbal ways.

It is important to eliminate barriers to participation when planning. For example, if your church or group has members with physical disabilities it is a good idea to ensure that materials and activities are placed at a suitable height. For others, you might wish to use a visual timetable to help an individual know what will be happening next and to show the choices that are available to them in the explore zones.

## Explore Together is a scary concept for our church. Is there any way we can implement it in stages?

The key to using Explore Together is to get to know and trust it. Using Explore Together in a smaller group setting to start with helps to build confidence and gets people involved. Using it in a house group setting or with a Sunday school group provides the ideal environment for becoming familiar with the process – children are so much more receptive to new ideas than adults!

I started using Explore Together with a small group of 5 to 11s. Other members of the children's team were involved and experienced first hand its effectiveness. From there we gained the confidence to share what we did in Sunday school with the wider church community. What started for me within a small group of children has now been used with 450 8 to 11-years-olds at Spring Harvest and in large national intergenerational events, too. If you need to, start small but don't be afraid to grow.

### How can Explore Together help adults who are reluctant to get out of the pew to engage?

The first thing to establish in situations like this is: Why the reluctance? If the reason concerns mobility and access then measures can be taken to make sure that all areas are easily available or, in extreme cases, the resources can be brought to the person.

More often than not the reluctance comes from the fear of change. The very nature of Explore Together is to provide an environment where every person can engage with the Bible in a way that embraces their natural preferences. There is quite literally something for everyone – the key is making sure that Explore Together is understood before it is forced upon a community that could be less than receptive.

If there are only one or two people for whom change may be difficult, take some time to sit down and explain what you plan to do and why you are doing it. There should be no pressure for people to go to a zone. One of the options is to reflect on the Bible passage quietly, and people could do this by staying in their seats; another is to deliver a sermon in the listening zone.

If the community is filled with people who are reluctant to leave their pews then maybe Explore Together in zone format is not right for you at this time. An alternative option would be to provide a bag (brown paper takeaway bags are ideal) for each person. The bag would contain a small notebook, a pen, a pack of coloured pencils, a small tub of play dough, some images relating to the Bible passage, a copy of the Bible passage or a Bible and a copy of the questions. The process would be the same, except that the community remains seated while they explore. The sharing time would be with those seated around them, and the feedback would happen in the same way as in the original format. This is less than ideal but it could be a stepping stone.

There will need to be a point at which a decision to move forward needs to be taken. Explore Together is a tool created to encourage people to discover the truths of the Bible for themselves. It is another pathway to a deeper relationship with God, intended to help people grow in their faith and reach maturity. Reluctance to engage should be seen as a pastoral opportunity to come alongside that person; to identify barriers and begin to break them down with prayer and persistence. Discipleship is never a done deal, it is a continuous journey that needs to take place in community. It also requires us to address and not ignore telltale signs that indicate the need for intervention – part of being a biblical community is to take that responsibility seriously (Colossians 1:28; 3:16). Explore Together helps to identify where on that journey we are and where help is needed.

### What if someone says something completely off-the-wall?

My immediate response to this question is, 'it's better out than in'. What better place is there to explore your faith and ask your questions than in a community of faith – a community made up of many people with varying levels of understanding, wisdom, knowledge and experience? Explore Together provides a safe environment for people to express their thoughts and ideas, some of which may otherwise never be aired or challenged. The questions help to provide safe boundaries and keep the focus on the desirable aims and outcomes.

**The web resources for the sessions in this book are available from:**
www.exploretogether.org/downloads

**Your access code is:** r4NG5eXP4Re8